# OUT OF THIS WORLD

**Fabulous Rhymes**

Edited By Jenni Harrison

First published in Great Britain in 2020 by:

Young Writers
Remus House
Coltsfoot Drive
Peterborough
PE2 9BF
Telephone: 01733 890066
Website: www.youngwriters.co.uk

All Rights Reserved
Book Design by Ashley Janson
© Copyright Contributors 2020
Softback ISBN 978-1-80015-016-4

Printed and bound in the UK by BookPrintingUK
Website: www.bookprintinguk.com
YB0446U

# FOREWORD

Here at Young Writers our defining aim is to promote the joys of reading and writing to children and young adults and we are committed to nurturing the creative talents of the next generation. By allowing them to see their own work in print we believe their confidence and love of creative writing will grow.

*Out Of This World* is our latest fantastic competition, specifically designed to encourage the writing skills of primary school children through the medium of poetry. From the high quality of entries received, it is clear that it really captured the imagination of all involved.

We are proud to present the resulting collection of poems that we are sure will amuse and inspire.

An absorbing insight into the imagination and thoughts of the young, we hope you will agree that this fantastic anthology is one to delight the whole family again and again.

# CONTENTS

**Independent Entries**

James Kinsella — 1

**Bersted Green Primary School, Bognor Regis**

Nadia Chojnacka (10) — 2
Sebastian Nowak (9) — 3

**Cann Hall Primary School, Clacton-On-Sea**

Harrison Silve (9) — 4

**Christ Church CEP Academy, Folkestone**

Mya Akuffo-Kelly (9) — 5

**Compass Pott Row, King's Lynn**

Riley Bloom (7) — 6
Georgie Stansfield (7) — 7

**Courthouse Junior School, Maidenhead**

Brooke Cudworth (8) — 8

**Ennerdale CE Primary School, Ennerdale Bridge**

Marcus Dean (10) — 9

**Frimley CE Junior School, Frimley Green**

Muhammad Yousaf (8) — 10
Lexi Dover (10) — 11
Noah Darby (7) — 12
Mia Searle (8) — 13
Amberley Wilcox (7) — 14

**Giggleswick Primary School, Giggleswick**

Daniel Griffin (8) — 15
Lily Marsden-Mellin — 16
Carl Sanderson (9) — 17

**Headlands Primary School, Northampton**

Anna Wilcox (11) — 18

**Kentisbeare CE Primary School, Kentisbeare**

Daisy Lush (7) — 20
Georgia Lewis (8) — 21

**Leweston Prep School, Leweston**

Arthur Ray (8) — 22
Tabitha Buchan-Moore (8) — 23
Sadie Littlechild (8) — 24
Harvey Wynne-Griffiths (8) — 25
Martha Murphy (8) — 26
Mia Pomeroy (7) — 27
Alice Master (8) — 28
Lucy Crowhurst (8) — 29

| | |
|---|---|
| Poppy Strainge (8) | 30 |
| Cecelia Bruce (8) | 31 |
| Oliver McAdorey (8) | 32 |
| Juliet King (9) | 33 |
| Florence Roberts (8) | 34 |
| Seb Baker (7) | 35 |

## Padstow Primary School, Padstow

| | |
|---|---|
| Amber Shephard (10) | 36 |
| Bethany Green (10) | 37 |

## Rosary Catholic Primary School, Stroud

| | |
|---|---|
| Laura Russell (10) | 38 |
| Taius Rooney (10) | 40 |
| Nicole Hudson (10) | 42 |
| Clara Bermingham (10) | 43 |
| Ida Synan (7) | 44 |
| Francis Bermingham (8) | 45 |

## Ryhall CE Academy, Ryhall

| | |
|---|---|
| Luke Fender (9) | 46 |
| Leila Porter-Toufik (9) | 47 |
| Isla Holroyd (9) | 48 |
| Robbie McIntosh (10) | 49 |
| Luisella Pacitti (9) | 50 |
| Lydia Sergeant (10) | 51 |
| Evie Linnell (9) | 52 |
| Anna Steel (10) | 53 |
| Mary-Ann Dawkins (9) | 54 |
| Faye Favell (10) | 55 |

## St Anthony's School For Girls, Golders Green

| | |
|---|---|
| Esther Thompson (8) | 56 |
| Amy Lee (7) | 57 |
| Eliana Rubin (8) | 58 |
| Edore Irikefe (7) | 59 |
| Alex Koryagin (8) | 60 |
| Isabella Ferraioli Putnis (7) | 61 |

| | |
|---|---|
| Alice Farrell (8) | 62 |
| Aavanya Arya (7) | 63 |

## St Francis De Sales RC Junior School, Tottenham

| | |
|---|---|
| Katherine Nwabuko (9) | 64 |
| Andrews John (9) | 65 |
| Adanna Onyearugbulem (9) | 66 |

## St Gerard's RC Primary School, Castle Vale

| | |
|---|---|
| Kian T (8) | 67 |
| Julia Lachendro (7) | 68 |

## St Peter's Catholic First School, Bromsgrove

| | |
|---|---|
| Maja Sliwa (9) | 69 |
| Jack O | 70 |
| Emelia T (9) | 72 |
| Emily Hodgson (9) | 73 |
| Lena Van Eijck (9) | 74 |
| Victoria Higgins (9) | 75 |
| Summer Kelly (9) | 76 |
| Emelia R (9) | 77 |
| Jack W | 78 |
| Martha Ranford (9) | 79 |
| Roke (9) | 80 |
| Alfie Hawkins (8) | 81 |
| Poppy Wells (8) | 82 |
| Dorris Freeman (9) | 83 |
| Martha Armitage (8) | 84 |
| Lily Nickless (9) | 85 |
| Finn Donnelly Smith (9) | 86 |
| Zoe Pratt (9) | 87 |
| Billie-Rose Juggins (8) | 88 |

## St Richard Reynolds Catholic College, Twickenham

| | |
|---|---|
| Esme Stewart (8) | 89 |
| Elsie Kinch (9) | 90 |
| Lou Belloc (9) | 92 |
| Amelia Nottage (8) | 93 |
| Bosley Brown (10) | 94 |
| Clemmie Needs (8) | 95 |
| Alessandro Gasparini (8) | 96 |
| Lucy Enfys Enfys Birdseye (8) | 97 |
| Finbar Harris (10) | 98 |
| Sienna Minhas (9) | 99 |
| Elisabeth Buxton (9) | 100 |
| Julia Szewczyk (9) | 101 |
| Liana Minhas (9) | 102 |
| Theo Corth (10) | 103 |
| Milo Ketteringham (9) | 104 |
| Annabelle Denizi (9) | 105 |
| Liam Pendleton (8) | 106 |
| Vic Mundow (9) | 107 |
| Luke Doyle (9) | 108 |
| Euan John Fitzgerald-Monk (9) | 109 |
| James Hazerd (9) | 110 |
| Jemima Larmour (8) | 111 |
| Lily Rae Inch (9) | 112 |

## St Stephen's Catholic Primary School, Skipton

| | |
|---|---|
| Marcus Hall (10) | 113 |

## Stoke Park Primary School, Lockleaze

| | |
|---|---|
| Oliver Butt (10) | 114 |
| Matilda Stringer (10) | 116 |
| Teodor Mehedinti (10) | 118 |
| Alexis Hildich-Flay (10) | 119 |
| Georgia Lewis (9) | 120 |
| Taylor Morris (10) | 122 |
| Taja Thomas (10) | 123 |
| Leo Lloyd (9) | 124 |
| Ronnie Steele (10) | 125 |

| | |
|---|---|
| Courtney-Anne Slane (10) | 126 |
| William Butt (9) | 127 |
| Matt Hardy (9) | 128 |

## Tany's Dell Primary School & Nursery, Harlow

| | |
|---|---|
| Dominic Norris (10) | 129 |
| Zoe Beck (9) | 130 |
| Amber Mitchell (10) | 132 |
| Homam Eizeddin (9) | 133 |
| Summer Parkin (9) | 134 |
| Lili Mai Turner (10) | 135 |
| Mark White (10) | 136 |
| Nathan Madge (9) | 137 |
| Lottie Waites (9) | 138 |
| Darcy Rowlandson (10) | 139 |
| Ruby Kings (10) | 140 |
| Beau Cruickshank (9) | 141 |
| Chloe Nash (9) | 142 |
| Jack Wiggins (9) | 143 |
| Alex Theodorou (9) | 144 |
| Abigail Jones (9) | 145 |
| Sophia Mckenzie (10) | 146 |
| Daisy Smiins (10) | 147 |
| Teegan Ayers (9) | 148 |
| Oliver Telfer-Maleary (10) | 149 |
| Logan Hodgson (9) | 150 |
| Lacie Arrowsmith | 151 |
| Ronnie Fry (9) | 152 |
| Keira Rooney (9) | 153 |
| Ruby Richardson (9) | 154 |
| Renée Smith (10) | 155 |
| Marcus Myers Evans (10) | 156 |
| Charlie Collier (9) | 157 |

## Temple Mill Primary School, Strood

| | |
|---|---|
| Ava Lane (8) | 158 |

## Turners Hill CE Primary School, Turners Hill

Watkins (9)                  159

## Wivelsfield Primary School, Wivelsfield

Jessica Meadows (9)        160

## Yorkmead Primary School, Hall Green

| | |
|---|---|
| Ilyas Widrig (8) | 161 |
| Krishna Tank (9) | 162 |
| Kritika Tank (9) | 163 |

# THE POEMS

# Jane

*In Loving Memory of Jane Elizabeth Kinsella 1st July 1958 - 2nd June 2013*

As spring gives way to summer
There will be lots of roses in bloom
But a rose blooms but once then dies
Those that are picked will wither and die in a short time
Those that are not picked will grow strong and beautiful
But they too will die with the coming of the fall
You are an unpacked rose in full bloom
That will never fade or die
The most beautiful rose in England.

**James Kinsella**

# Horses

My name is Lash
I'm as quick as a flash
I love to run
Up and down
My beautiful mane
White-sea mane
Clop clop clop clop
Ride over the hill
The night is still
Clop clop clop clop
I can hear
So good and delicate
Over the hill
Clop clop clop clop
I can hear.

## Nadia Chojnacka (10)
Bersted Green Primary School, Bognor Regis

# Gladiators

Down in the garden in the open grass
Two gladiators were battling each other
Jumping one by one
There wasn't a giant battle area
It was only grass but...
They didn't have shiny helmets
Or gazing golden armour
Because they were only chickens!

## Sebastian Nowak (9)
Bersted Green Primary School, Bognor Regis

# The Life Of A Dinosaur

Dinosaurs are bloodthirsty, brutal, distinctive animals. They might not live today but there is a lot of evidence to suggest they lived on this very planet. These bloody brutal animals lived at the very start of the beginning. We can tell these creatures once lived because of the evidence from the fossils.

Did you know that dinosaurs first started in 0 BC when God was still creating the world? The vegetarians like the diplodocus looked cute but they were brutal! They had to kill to survive. Around 2000 million years later they became extinct because a massive meteor flew into the world. Did God do this on purpose?

## Harrison Silve (9)
Cann Hall Primary School, Clacton-On-Sea

# Summer

Summer is here so let's have a cheer
So much fun running in the sun
Picking up sand with your hand
Never foggy or boggy
Because it's summer!

Riding bikes, flat tyres
Charging phones and very long wires
Eating food like fish and chips
Getting vinegar all over your lips
Because it's summer!

**Mya Akuffo-Kelly (9)**
Christ Church CEP Academy, Folkestone

# The Colours Of Harry Potter

Red is the blood from Harry fighting Voldemort
Yellow reminds me of the Hufflepuff badger
Blue is the colour of Ravenclaw, they are clever
Green is the nature in the trees in the Forbidden Forest
White is the colour of Nearly Headless Nick the ghost
Black is the colour of cloaks.

### Riley Bloom (7)
Compass Pott Row, King's Lynn

# The Colours Of Magic

Blue is the colour of the sky at Hogwarts
Red is the colour of Voldemort's heart
Green is the colour of the grass at Hogwarts
Black is the colour of the night sky at Hogwarts
Yellow is the colour of Hufflepuff
White is the colour of snow at Christmas.

**Georgie Stansfield (7)**
Compass Pott Row, King's Lynn

# Dreams

Dreams are special
Dreams are there
Dreams aren't perfect
But you have to be aware

Dreams come and go
Even if you know
That dreams can be bad
Don't be sad

Even if you know
That dreams can go
Please don't cry
'Cause dreams can't die

You can get what you want
But sometimes not
So you have to believe
In what you've got.

**Brooke Cudworth (8)**
Courthouse Junior School, Maidenhead

# Remembrance

R ed scarlet poppies on your dark, gloomy winter coat
E veryone remembers the strong, tough soldiers who died in the war
M en died in the dangerous bloody war, to fight for their country to win
E choing guns shooting down below the windy stormy day
M en risked their lives going into the dry, hot deserts to fight
B rothers and sisters and husbands went out to the violent bloody war
R isking their lives for their countries to beat the Germans
A lways we will remember the people who fought for our country and died
N obody should ever forget the brave, tough soldiers who were fighting
C an you imagine how brave they must have been?
E very year we wear our bright red poppies with happy heartfelt pride.

## Marcus Dean (10)
Ennerdale CE Primary School, Ennerdale Bridge

# A Honey Attack

As I woke up on a bright sunny day
My mum calls me down, "Hey,
Breakfast is ready."
I question, "Mum, what about Freddie?"
My toast bounces out, staring at me
I can hear they say, "Eat me! Eat me!"
I forget about my brother Freddie
And reach out for the legendary honey
This honey is made from special bees
From a faraway land across the seven seas
It tastes of chocolate mixed with toffee
And is the perfect combination with my creamy coffee
I spread it over my toasted bread
Still calling my brother Fred
He comes down the stairs into the dining room
Grabs my toast, runs off, and trips over the broom
I shout horribly, "I want my toast back!"
Mum looks at me having a heart attack
I spin around and drizzle her mouth with honey
She calms down and says, "You really are a pair of funny bunnies."

## Muhammad Yousaf (8)
Frimley CE Junior School, Frimley Green

# The World Of Small

Imagine a place, not space but small
It's the complete opposite of everything and all
Imagine no hunger, it's full of fruit
Need to breathe, no need for a suit
Imagine the world of small!

Imagine the land white not black
On the moon it's not just a shack
There are buildings and people everywhere!
This is a place for those who care
Imagine the world of small!

If you think it's fake
Go stare at a lake and watch the animals die
If you start to feel you care
Start to make your way up there
Go to the world of small!

## Lexi Dover (10)
Frimley CE Junior School, Frimley Green

# I Am A Dragon!

I am a dragon
And my tail is as long as a mouse
No not a mouse, a house!

I am a dragon
And my eyes are as blue as the sky

I am a dragon
And my wings make me fly
As gracefully as a ballerina

I am a dragon
And my spikes are as sharp as spears!

I am a dragon
And my deadly teeth are as white as clouds

I am a dragon
And my horns are as orange as fire!

I am a...
Malevolent and evil dragon
And I'm going to...
Eat you!

**Noah Darby (7)**
Frimley CE Junior School, Frimley Green

# Someone Stood On My Paper

Someone stood on my paper
It made me feel really sad
But it helped me think of a poem minutes later
So I didn't feel so mad

There's a big footprint on my page
So it looks all old and tired
It put me in a big rage
How do I turn this into something to be admired?

It was a boy in Year Five
Who ruined my competition entry
He is lucky I let him walk away alive
As it was me who dropped it on the floor, I decided to let him be.

**Mia Searle (8)**
Frimley CE Junior School, Frimley Green

# My Dream Dragon

One quiet day a boy strolled through the woods. From a distance he heard a strange, ear-piercing roar. With excitement the boy's heart beat as fast as a cheetah. He hoped it could be his dream dragon. As fast as he could he ran to the noise. His impatience to be there nearly caused him to tumble. He stopped, broken-hearted, as he found a small statue of a young baby dragon eating his food. A sound from behind made him quiver with fear, in his mind he knew a real dragon was near.

**Amberley Wilcox (7)**
Frimley CE Junior School, Frimley Green

# Super Turtle

In Petropolis was Super Turtle.

Super Turtle saves the day,
Super Turtle hip hip hooray!

Super Turtle hides from villains,
Then sneaks out and sends them to prison!

Super Turtle loves to eat,
It makes him strong but he has treats.

He flies in the sky for a good look about,
He beats up heroes and is a hero.

For the last verse let's have a final hooray,
For Super Turtle saves the big parade. Hip hip hooray!

## Daniel Griffin (8)
Giggleswick Primary School, Giggleswick

# Aliens

Aliens do not love anything
Aliens do not love underpants, they do not like them.
Aliens hate cats, dogs and any animals
Some aliens are allergic.
Aliens hate you and me.
Aliens do not like chocolate.
Aliens do not like anything!
Aliens love deep, dark space.

**Lily Marsden-Mellin**
Giggleswick Primary School, Giggleswick

# A Day In Space

Up, up and away I go
In a rocket shooting above the stars
The furious hissing sounds of the jets in fast flow
What will I discover when I land on the moon?
I hope a magical glittering palace.

**Carl Sanderson (9)**
Giggleswick Primary School, Giggleswick

# My School Is NOT Normal!

There are mermaids in the corridors,
Monsters in the halls,
Toilet seats below the stairs,
Hamsters in the walls,

The teachers are no better,
They're all guinea pigs,
You can't write with the pencils,
They're all broken twigs!

Row, row, row your boat,
Slowly through the roof,
All the writing books,
Vanish with a poof!

Don't get the school dinners,
If you don't like mouldy fruit!
The playground's filled with pirates,
Looking for new loot,

Row, row, row your boat,
Slowly through my school,
If you look quite carefully,
You will see them all!

**Anna Wilcox (11)**
Headlands Primary School, Northampton

# Me And My Minnie Lop Rabbit Scooby Doo

A little tiny rabbit in my arms,
Best friends forever.
He's got big bulging eyes and big floppy ears
With cute little whiskers and a tiny little nose!
He's a good little rabbit and is cute.
I adore him in every way possible.
He twitches his nose like he is a detective.
Everyone loves him as he is a baby.
He is 12 weeks, how cute!
He's the best pet in the world.
He needs love and care, all by me!

## Daisy Lush (7)
Kentisbeare CE Primary School, Kentisbeare

# Friends

F is for Freya
R is for Ruby
I is for Immi
E is for Ellie
N is for nothing can stop us
D is for doing stuff together.

## Georgia Lewis (8)
Kentisbeare CE Primary School, Kentisbeare

# The Space Dragon

I ran outside and looked up high
What can I see in the sky?
I am staring into the night
I can see the stars shining bright.
First I see two mighty wings
They look like two big flapping things
Then I spot his tail and pointed claws
I peer along his body and make out his head and jaws.
The dragon constellation is very shiny
Made up of thousands of stars that are tiny
The stars sparkle, he appears to me alive
And I cannot believe my eyes.
He looks so fun and playful
Watch the dragon, he's wonderful
Every morning the sun comes up and he is gone
I decided to call him my Space Dragon.

## Arthur Ray (8)
Leweston Prep School, Leweston

# My Crazy Family

I live in a family of six
In a big house made entirely of bricks
I have three lazy big brothers
And one wonderful, slightly crazy mother
One lovely father
Whom I would rather
Did not make a joke
Every time that he spoke
Two huge, hairy doggies
And four cute little moggies
They love to eat
But can be often found fast asleep!
I have four little guineas
Who eat so much they aren't skinny
And then, of course, there's me
Who Mummy says is as sweet as can be.

**Tabitha Buchan-Moore (8)**
Leweston Prep School, Leweston

# Cola Cola Cola

Cola is the name of our dog,
She likes a big, muddy bog.
My doggy's name is Cola,
Or Cola Cola Cola Lola.
She is a Lagotto,
With a motto.
She would go on a walk,
But she is not able to talk.
She is so funny,
And she would like to chase a bunny.
She is like a beaver,
Luckily she doesn't have a fever.
She loves ham,
But hates Spam.
She likes to chew a bone,
When she's at home.
That's our dog, Cola.

## Sadie Littlechild (8)
Leweston Prep School, Leweston

# My Family Through The Stars

In my bedroom there stands a telescope,
Accessed on a platform with a rope,
I gaze at the galaxy up so high
I can see my whole family in the sky,
Gemini is Milo, both angel and devil at once,
There's Taurus, my daddy,
Stubborn and strong (but don't ask him to dance!)
Scorpio my mummy,
She loves me without fail,
But watch out for the nasty sting in her tail!
And lastly, there I am,
Sagittarius, the half-horse man in the sky.

**Harvey Wynne-Griffiths (8)**
Leweston Prep School, Leweston

# In The Night-Time Sky

In the night-time sky all is dark
You need to do art
And go on your knees
But then you will freeze

In the night-time sky
You're afraid to die
You don't want to die
Whilst wearing a tie

In the night-time sky
You might fry
Although you're looking at the sky
You don't know why but you don't like looking at the sky

In the night-time sky
Like a moth in the sky but I try to fly.

**Martha Murphy (8)**
Leweston Prep School, Leweston

# Our Planets

**U** ranus, the seventh planet from the sun
**N** eptune is the eighth and farthest planet from the sun
**I** n the distance the stars are glistening and gleaming
**V** enus is named after the Roman goddess of love
**E** arth formed over 4.5 billion years ago
**R** evolve around the sun in the same direction
**S** aturn is the second largest planet in the solar system
**E** ath's molten iron core creates a magnetic field.

## Mia Pomeroy (7)
Leweston Prep School, Leweston

# Glue Stick Pritt Stick

I love to glue with a Pritt Stick,
I do it all day long.
I love to glue with a Pritt Stick,
Because it reminds me of a song.

I love to glue with a Pritt Stick,
I would glue up all my friends.
I love to glue with a Pritt Stick,
And see them standing on ends.

When I grow up I want to be a fireman,
So I can glue up the hose.
I want to make a glue stick,
That smells like a rose.

## Alice Master (8)
Leweston Prep School, Leweston

# Dive Into The World Of Stars!

Please star, please star come out to shine your light
Don't be afraid, I'm your friend
I see you above, peeping through the misty cloud
I know it's cold but be bold
And leave that comforting cloud

Stop feeling shy, you are so very high
It is getting darker and darker
The star is getting brighter and brighter
The star is finally out
Well done star!
I knew you could do it!

**Lucy Crowhurst (8)**
Leweston Prep School, Leweston

# My Piggy Peggy

Once there was a piggy that I named Peggy.
She lived on our farm which was called Carter's Barn.
We always talked on our long walks.
Peggy could be sensitive but also very inquisitive.
Peggy loved to find apples to munch and crunch.
She made a sloppy, soggy mess which went all over my dress!
The thing I liked to do most with Peggy was have a cuddle
And tickle her stubble which made me chuckle.

## Poppy Strainge (8)
Leweston Prep School, Leweston

# Cookies And Cream

Cookies and cream,
It's my favourite treat,
If you would like some then
Please take a seat
Cookies and cream can be anything,
Any ice cream,
Any dream,
Cold or hot,
I always have a lot,
It is just so chocolatey,
I'd rather have cookies and cream for my tea,
Yum yum, mmmmm, cookies and cream!

## Cecelia Bruce (8)
Leweston Prep School, Leweston

# Football

**F** eet hurt after a match
**O** liver was great
**O** ther players were not as good as he
**T** ournaments won were many
**B** all in the net
**A** lways happy during the match
**L** ong live Oliver - the greatest player in the world
**L** ong live football - the greatest sport in the world.

## Oliver McAdorey (8)
Leweston Prep School, Leweston

# Wonderful Winter

The frosty grass and crisp leaves set a cold but calm atmosphere,
Inside the fire crackles but the wind and snow is all I can hear.
As we have tea I take in the warmness of the apple pies,
But as we eat the wind and snow dies.
Then we continue to watch the snowflakes fall,
It is winter after all!

## Juliet King (9)
Leweston Prep School, Leweston

# Fancy A Trip?

Welcome to space,
Have you seen the beauty with your face?
Are you feeling excited
Because you are the one I invited?
You never know who we may see on Mars,
I hope you enjoy your trip through the stars,
Let's see if we can walk on the moon,
Don't worry, we will be back soon!

## Florence Roberts (8)
Leweston Prep School, Leweston

# Space

- **S** tars everywhere
- **P** lanets like Mars, Saturn, Jupiter
- **A** place to be amazed
- **C** urly rings on some planets
- **E** verywhere is incredible.

**Seb Baker (7)**
Leweston Prep School, Leweston

# Space Race

I'm going on a race to outer space
The aliens are furry, two-eyed or topsy-turvy
Round the rings of Saturn, ooh look there's a baton
When I went past Mars I could see the other cars
Behind the stars, there were monkey bars
In the distance, I could see the awesome pawsome pets
There were some mugs and inside there were pugs
On the moon it was noon
Look there's the finish line, just in time.

## Amber Shephard (10)
Padstow Primary School, Padstow

# Out Of Space

**O** ut of space, such a wondrous place
**U** p out of the atmosphere
**T** o another solar system

**O** ut of space, find out more
**F** or there are secrets you can discover

**S** omewhere there is another world
**P** ut your hope towards your dreams
**A** nd befriend other beings
**C** ome to Zarg and find out more
**E** very day we want to find out more.

## Bethany Green (10)
Padstow Primary School, Padstow

# Sublime Swifts Hill

We walk up there on Christmas Day
The slopes walk away from you
Yet you get there in the end

As still as statues for the wonder of it all
Your gasp's fingers stretch a mile
The world is wildly willing to declare
It will never end or if it does I may end

As in prehistoric times you can see the hills hugging you on all sides
Swaying trees are like hairs standing on the skin
Over many years, after tears and smiles, the carvings of houses has ended
The hills peacefully continue to harvest life

The air is fresh and pure to exhale, refreshingly calm to inhale
The sky-sea carries graceful fish
So strong to fall a house yet delicate as a radiant rose.

Through bramble and thicket you trudge
While giants' footsteps echo a path

The battered boards tell of hawks and mice
We find a more tranquil life within

The resplendent landscape is like a treasure box
When you find yourself up there you become a bird
Free, free, free
At the foot you feel kicked away

We walk up there on Christmas Day
The slopes walk away from you
Yet you get there in the end.

**Laura Russell (10)**
Rosary Catholic Primary School, Stroud

# The Bells

Fire is burning
The waters are blue
The bells ring out
But ring for who?

The earth is shaking
Violent and loud
The wind is blowing
Through the cities and clouds

Towers will topple
Proud mountains will too
The bells are ringing
But ring for who?

Animals flee
Humans do too
The bells are ringing
But ring for who?

The inferno starts
The flood begins
The tremors rumble

To herald high winds
Blazing, burning
Cracking, churning
Gushing, surging
Blowing, blasting
Crashing, clashing
Bashing too
The bells are ringing
But ring
For
Who?

## Taius Rooney (10)
Rosary Catholic Primary School, Stroud

# The Thing About Billy Is

The thing about Billy is
He scratches on the door to go out like a branch scratching a car
And scratches on the door to come in
I say, Billy
Send a text or ring the doorbell.

Another thing about Billy is
He always asks for food, like a baby crying at a library
I say, Billy
Think of your diet and think of your manners.

The final thing about Billy is
He wanders away with mates we've never met like a teenager
I say, Billy
I'm fine with that but don't forget me.

Billy has green eyes and freckles on his face
Just like my BFF Olivia.

## Nicole Hudson (10)
Rosary Catholic Primary School, Stroud

# Trees

Trees are what hold the world together.
They keep the planet green.
They produce lots of oxygen that keep our bodies clean.
Green leaves, flowers and bees, that's the best part.
Glowing in the summer, in winter covered in snow,
they are terrific, they make me smile.
Trees will never go out of style.
When the lights go down, they turn into a beautiful green gown,
that sways in the mellow breeze.
But when they are cut down, it makes me frown.
If we didn't have trees, the earth would drown.

## Clara Bermingham (10)
Rosary Catholic Primary School, Stroud

# The Martian's Point Of View

My loyal Martian friends, the Earth is a place full of boxes that those so-called people live in. They have boxes they call shops and have to tell a person what they have and give them so-called money. They have people that live on 'streets' and they call them homeless. They have people called scientists that discover all their technology. So Martian friends I hope you have learned Mars is better than Earth!

### Ida Synan (7)
Rosary Catholic Primary School, Stroud

# An Explore Around The Galaxy

Colliding, crashing
Meteors are zooming past
The coloured planets,
Stars shining in the distance,
The wondrous universe.

### Francis Bermingham (8)
Rosary Catholic Primary School, Stroud

# Food I Hate

There are some foods that I just don't rate
And some of them I positively hate!
One thing I could never devour,
Is the knobbly, nibbly cauliflower.
I couldn't stomach a teaspoon of mustard,
Yellow food should stop at custard.
I'm strangely averse to fizzy drinks
Or any food that truly stinks.
And just the thought of a plate of liver
Makes my insides go all of a quiver.
One thing that spoils a lovely cake
Is to add fruit into the bake
Gherkins and pickles make me shriek
And I would never venture to eat a leek.
So if you ever ask me to dinner
Avoid these foods and you're onto a winner!

**Luke Fender (9)**
Ryhall CE Academy, Ryhall

# A Country Stroll

I wandered down a lonely lane
A horse came by with a flowing mane
The sun was bright, the day was warm
I came upon a lovely farm

The sheep were there with lambs at play
It all made for a perfect day
The birds were singing so full of voice
Apart from this there was no noise

The cows were munching in the grass
The lake was still, it shone like glass
Farmers were busy making hay
The work ideal for a summer day

Fatigue set in, it was soon dark
From in the woods I heard a bark
So time for bed, I homeward strolled
As darkness fell, the air turned cold.

## Leila Porter-Toufik (9)
Ryhall CE Academy, Ryhall

# Wishing Spring Was Here

Short days, cold nights
Wrapped up in my winter warmers
Looking out my bedroom window
Wishing spring was here
I close my eyes and dream away
Spring is here let's celebrate
The sun is shining brightly
Birds are flying high
Weaving straw and feathers
Building nests for babies
Beautiful coloured daffodils
Smiling in the sunshine
The sound of children laughing
Playing in their gardens
Everyone having fun
Oh come on spring I wish you were here!

**Isla Holroyd (9)**
Ryhall CE Academy, Ryhall

# Fun Football

I woke to early rain coming down the drain, but I was happy because it was time to play football and not just to train.

Saturday is match day also known as my fun day. It's why we train every Tuesday, in any weather rain or shine.

When the ball comes to me I call, "Mine." I control the ball and I will just smack it into the top corner of the goal. But at the end of the day it is just a game. Whether we win or lose or even draw, having fun is our aim!

## Robbie McIntosh (10)
Ryhall CE Academy, Ryhall

# My Pet Worm, Bubblegum

**B** ubblegum is my soft and furry pet worm
**U** nder the bed, she sometimes squirms
**B** est friends are she and I
**B** oth of us curl up on my bean bag and watch the colours of the sky
**L** ighting up the world around us
**E** ven when my mum makes a fuss
**G** oing on and on at us to tidy our room
**U** nder my duvet, Bubblegum and I hide
**M** ischievously plotting our next adventure outside.

**Luisella Pacitti (9)**
Ryhall CE Academy, Ryhall

# The Mountain Climb

The icy breeze warms my heart
The crystal snow makes me smile
Slowly, slowly up the snow-capped mountain
The rocks tumbling down, down
Down after my every step
The icy breeze against my face
How much longer?
The snow feels like needles against my chest
If only they had not left me.

## Lydia Sergeant (10)
Ryhall CE Academy, Ryhall

# Horses

**H** andling horses is so much fun
**O** n top of my horse we run
**R** unning over hills and hollows
**S** topping somewhere to watch the swallows
**E** vie is my name, I love riding my horse
**S** topping for lunch after a hard day, of course!

### Evie Linnell (9)
Ryhall CE Academy, Ryhall

# My Adventure

One day I met a dog who lived in the fog. He slept on a log near somewhere puddly and muddy like a bog. His name was Zog.

Then I met a cat who slept on a mat. She was very fat, her unusual name was Bubbly Bat.

## Anna Steel (10)
Ryhall CE Academy, Ryhall

# My Beautiful Unicorn

Her skin as white as freshly fallen snow
Her eyes as blue as the clearest royal crystal sky
Her hair as colourful as the colossal bright rainbow
That's why I very much love my beautiful unicorn.

**Mary-Ann Dawkins (9)**
Ryhall CE Academy, Ryhall

# Family Forever

Family, family what keeps you safe
A family that holds lots of faith
Keeping us together will last forever
Whenever we're close our hearts will join together
To live forever.

**Faye Favell (10)**
Ryhall CE Academy, Ryhall

# Snow All Day Long

It's snowing today, it should all day long
Snowflakes fluttering in the cloudy sky
Snow falling down from the heavens above
Snow, snow, snow all day long

Snow everywhere on the streets
Children playing merrily with the snow
Little children building snowmen in the snow
They throw snowballs around the field, having fun in the cold weather

What a lovely snowy day
I wish it would snow every day
To watch little children playing in the snow
While it snows all day long.

## Esther Thompson (8)
St Anthony's School For Girls, Golders Green

# Gloria, The Biggest Star

My name is Gloria and I shine at night
I have a pointy end but I don't hurt you
And my favourite fruit is an apple
I can be very shiny like a movie star in the dark
I can be very shy in the light
And I can be found by a warm heart
And you can be as warm as an apple tart
When you are sad I can be your shooting star
When you are happy I can be the biggest star
I can be your sky and you can be my star
I am Gloria, the biggest star.

## Amy Lee (7)
St Anthony's School For Girls, Golders Green

# The Secret Solar System

The giant, fiery sun is our queen
She's the biggest thing I have ever seen!

Surrounded by galaxies
There are some tragedies

Mesmerising Mercury that's who I am
I've never been reached by any man

I'm serious Saturn
You will learn

My rocky rings
Oh those old things

The giant fiery sun is our queen
She is the biggest thing I have ever seen!

**Eliana Rubin (8)**
St Anthony's School For Girls, Golders Green

# My Greek Holiday

I played in the sun with my sister and it was a lot of fun.
I went in the pool, splashed and it was very cool.
I ordered some food and it was exceedingly good.
My family and me paddling in the big blue sea.
I walked over to see a show and the stage was aglow.
White party in the sand and it was grand.
Bikini and then hiking, that's what I'm liking.
Ancient tomb and staying up to see the red moon.

## Edore Irikefe (7)
St Anthony's School For Girls, Golders Green

# The Friendly Monster

Once upon a time, there was a monster called Mike
He lived with his parents called Mr and Mrs Light.
He always dreamt about riding a bike
Or having some friends to play through the night.
One evening, when Mike was going to bed
He felt very lonely and very sad.
He went to the window and there was a shocking bicycle
Mrs Light was silently carrying one through the moonlight!

## Alex Koryagin (8)
St Anthony's School For Girls, Golders Green

# The Talking Moon

Once there was a talking moon
That was singing a tune
"I live in outer space
And this is my favourite place
Space is very beautiful
And that is why I am suitable
Last night when I was talking to Mars
He said that I look like stars!
Then I went to Saturn
And he said he liked my pattern!"
And that was the tune
Of the moon.

## Isabella Ferraioli Putnis (7)
St Anthony's School For Girls, Golders Green

# Beautiful Space

*Haiku poetry*

The vacuum of space
Millions of stars and lights
I wish to be there

Floating around space
Where has the gravity gone?
I left it on Earth!

Orbiting planets
Spinning around the hot sun
All of them unique.

## Alice Farrell (8)
St Anthony's School For Girls, Golders Green

# Robots Over The World

Robots, robots over the world
We need help, people, robots are everywhere
What are we going to do?
Watch out, people!
We need more people to help us
Please, please help us!
We need help
Robots are finishing our future!

### Aavanya Arya (7)
St Anthony's School For Girls, Golders Green

# When I Grow Up

A ll my jobs are amazing but I want to be an astronomer
S tars shine bright like a diamond
T he solar system's larger than an island
R ockets at the ready, the blast is never silent
O n Jupiter the moons are always reliant
N eptune isn't too far from Jupiter, as you may know, it's a giant
O nly comets and meteors can fly through space
M any thanks to the astronauts that have graced us from their space base
E vents in the solar system are what puts a smile on my face
R emember our galaxy is important, it's such a beautiful place.

**Katherine Nwabuko (9)**
St Francis De Sales RC Junior School, Tottenham

# Nightmares

Bad thoughts crawling in my head
As I lay down in my bed
My eyes close shut
Sleeping began
With nightmares in my head

Skeletons with bows and arrows
Zombies zombifying animals
Horses with no heads
Humans with no legs
All of these are nightmares

Dreams of old battlefields
Ghosts yielding swords and shields
The undead coming alive
Monster armies in rows of forty-five
All of these are nightmares

Gruesome, scary, very crazy horror
Give you terror
These are my nightmares.

## Andrews John (9)
St Francis De Sales RC Junior School, Tottenham

# Home And Home To Stay

**H** ome is where I roam and keep warm
**O** n my bed I lie warm
**M** y home sweet home is where I roam
**E** ven when cold I'm always warm in my home sweet home

Home is the place where I'm snug in my bed
Where I lie comfortably asking for bread
Home, home, wherever I roam
I've always been home.

## Adanna Onyearugbulem (9)
St Francis De Sales RC Junior School, Tottenham

# Double Deluxe

Today I am getting a Burger Deluxe
I'm doing this to burst the sky
*Boom! Pop! Bash!*
Then while in the sky
The trees will wave goodbye
When I am eating my burger up
My belly will grow until it can't anymore
But I will save all the space for my giant Burger Deluxe taste
Can I even fill it up for next time?
Maybe I could, maybe I couldn't
I think I'll grow to eat it again
Maybe next time I might eat a double Deluxe
I'll eat it all again until I don't live again.

## Kian T (8)
St Gerard's RC Primary School, Castle Vale

# Burgers

Burgers smell so nice
They taste so yummy
I won't say yuck
They are like flowery perfume
They are so good
Better than anything else in the world!

### Julia Lachendro (7)
St Gerard's RC Primary School, Castle Vale

# The Big Explosion

Trying to get out
She rumbles with her ruby-red lava
In the city, the tired donkeys are slowly clip-clopping across the town
Any time she can explode with her boiling hot lava
This volcano is sleepy and angry, scary too
Out of the underground, she bursts out with a shivery blast
People shouting with fear
Scared but amused they shout
Deadly the cloud covers the town
Gas kills the people that hide in their homes
People have no strength against the big volcano
The bad luck finally came
She cries with her lava but still she lets her horrible deadly ash out
Nobody survives, dead bodies sleep underground
With horrifying, deadly memories.

## Maja Sliwa (9)
St Peter's Catholic First School, Bromsgrove

# Pompeii Disaster

Under their feet he rumbled
WIth his steaming, corrosive mantle
Around the bustling giant town people busy
With their gleaming, valuable money
Out the door, someone shouts
"Come buy ripe fruit and fresh bread!"
Deep underground, the mantle flows
Nobody knows how it will go...

On the floor, things start to shake
Tall, fragile buildings start to fall
Heading to the city fly the keen, white-hot rocks
People scream, "Get out of the house!"
Down the volcano the crimson, disruptive lava flows
Taking over things that nobody knows
In the air rocks collide
Making swift, perilous lightning bolts.

Five hundred years later, Pompeii was rediscovered
Looking like an ancient unknown city
After this eruption he sleeps

Feeling sorrowful about his super savage attack
All over the world people visit Pompeii
Remembering the upsetting sudden story
Nobody knows if this could happen again.

## Jack O
St Peter's Catholic First School, Bromsgrove

# Mount Vesuvius

Deep down in her stomach lay the boiling hot lava
Down in Pompeii, the citizens stood
Waiting for kind, loving family and friends
But as much fun as they were having
A humongous volcano was about to erupt out of its crater
Soon booming and bursting lava with grey heavy rocks
Was shooting out of its crater and landing all over the city
When the lava landed on the ground
It turned bubbly, crimson red
Down the slope, the fiery lava went
With hard, hot rocks and stone
Hundreds of years later, with her molten hot lava
Locked up inside her stomach
After the eruption the citizens froze
Covered in thick smooth ash and pumice stone.

### Emelia T (9)
St Peter's Catholic First School, Bromsgrove

# Pompeii

On a little island the people were selling
Near to the massive, dangerous volcano
Out of nowhere she cried
And the massive, grey slopes started to shake
Down underground she rumbles
With her humongous fat stomach

Around the corner, people screamed
As the fiery, bright volcano erupted
All of a sudden she burst out
Monstrous violent lightning
Over the crater she lurked
A grey, astonishing ash cloud

Hundreds of years later plants grow
With their green fascinating stems
Locked inside her, she sleeps
WIth her molten, fiery lava
In the distance she rests
Like a tired, rusty person.

## Emily Hodgson (9)
St Peter's Catholic First School, Bromsgrove

# Mount Vesuvius

Over by the calm lake he guards
His magnificent, outstanding city
Across the sturdy bridge he shakes
His precious light head
Nearby the mountains he bursts
His violent, deadly lava
Around the corner he slithers
Out his boiling, dangerous crater
In the distance he sways
His venomous, gloomy eruption cloud
Next to the houses he covers
The lost forgotten city
Over by the mountains Pompeii lies
Covered with deadly, dusty ash.

### Lena Van Eijck (9)
St Peter's Catholic First School, Bromsgrove

# Pompeii's Doom!

Below the rocky ground
She feels a rumbling in her belly
Ready to erupt out her steaming, deadly lava
Underground, the volcano is getting oozy
As the deadly lava gets hotter and hotter
As the pressure builds up
Gushing out of the volcano
Deadly hot lava spraying up in the air
With her crimson lava
In twenty-four hours the city of Pompeii
Is covered in hot deadly lava
Not one building showing
Covered in ash and lava.

## Victoria Higgins (9)
St Peter's Catholic First School, Bromsgrove

# Pompeii

In Pompeii the ground shakes mysteriously, ferociously, never-ending.
In the city, Mount Vesuvius sleeps as people calmly, unworriedly shop.
By the tall houses the ground shakes as the volcano erupts.
Bursting out of the crater, she surges out her thick bubbly lava.
Into the sky, rises her deadly, foggy smoke.
Buried, people choke under cooled, thick lava.
Hundreds of years later, people discover the innocent, terrified people of Pompeii.

**Summer Kelly (9)**
St Peter's Catholic First School, Bromsgrove

# Pompeii

Rumbling violently over the island
Wiggles Mount Vesuvius
Rocks sensibly began to rumble
Booming loudly, she cries her crimson lava
Rapidly her tears flow down her cheek
A bunch of pitch-black smoke
Pompeii invaded by black terrifying smoke
It's unhealthy for them
Over 100 people died and two people survived
It's now covered in ash and dust
It's sad.

### Emelia R (9)
St Peter's Catholic First School, Bromsgrove

# The Erupting Volcano

Deep down in her stomach lies the steaming hot magma
In Pompeii the volcano lies above the joyful, playful city
When the lava slithered down the slope it crackled and popped
The destructive and monstrous lava crawled down the endless road of people
After the eruption she watches her molten crumbly lava
After the eruption she regrets erupting
What a horrible volcano she is.

## Jack W
St Peter's Catholic First School, Bromsgrove

# Mount Vesuvius

On the island he shows
His strong, powerful body
Under the summer ground he shakes
His colossal, solid rock
In the Italian sea he shoots
His scorching amber fireballs
Ground hugging, he spreads
His raging harmful lava
In the city he swoops
His black, dusty eruption cloud
Deep below the ground he covers
His doddery, damaged Pompeii.

## Martha Ranford (9)
St Peter's Catholic First School, Bromsgrove

# Pompeii Eruption

Next to the city of Pompeii he lies asleep
With his oozing, deadly lava
In Pompeii people shop
With their bronze, shining money
Blasting out of the crater
He exploded out with his crimson, destructive lava
Citizens running, scared citizens
Millions of years later he sleeps
With his fiery raging red-hot lava
Over Pompeii.

## Roke (9)
St Peter's Catholic First School, Bromsgrove

# Pompeii

In Pompeii, their great protector
Mount Vesuvius erupted
His flaming, roasting lava started to come out
More and more lava came
And Mount Vesuvius got angrier and angrier
That is when people started to pass out
Nearly everyone started to pass out
Because of the gas
The people in the houses had no idea
What had happened.

## Alfie Hawkins (8)
St Peter's Catholic First School, Bromsgrove

# Mount Vesuvius

Around the corner she guards
Her happy, beautiful town
Deep beneath she shakes
Her large, rumbly earth
By the volcano she pops out
Her rolling, quick lava
Aside the volcano she shoots out
Her burning hot lava
In the sky she swirls
Her pitch-black eruption cloud
In the horizon she covers
Her empty lost town.

**Poppy Wells (8)**
St Peter's Catholic First School, Bromsgrove

# Mount Vesuvius

In the distance stood a jolly, caring town
Over in Pompeii he wobbled the horrifying, dangerous ground
Inside he bubbled, he was a hot, steamy volcano!
Bubbling in the sky, he explodes
His hot, smoky lava
High in the sky, he spreads
Fierce, toxic venom
Under the volcanic soil lies a forgotten, ruined Pompeii.

## Dorris Freeman (9)
St Peter's Catholic First School, Bromsgrove

# Escape Pompeii

As the earth cracks they listen
To the loud terrified screams
Above the sea
They cough out their thick, blasting mist
As the lava bursts up
It runs towards the huge busy city
As the lava runs down the slope
Smoke flies through the busy, hot Pompeii
Down the slope they spit out their red-hot lava.

## Martha Armitage (8)
St Peter's Catholic First School, Bromsgrove

# Mount Vesuvius

Far away she guards
Her pretty amazing town
In the town she shakes
She horribly, dastardly topples over
Next to the town she stands
She splurts out deadly burning lava
Swirling in the sky she swerves
Her toxic, gloomy ash
Under a blanket of ash she slumps
Her shattered, destroyed town.

**Lily Nickless (9)**
St Peter's Catholic First School, Bromsgrove

# Mount Vesuvius

Up high he drooled
His hot molten lava
Over the hills he flew
His pitch-dark cloud
In the distance he rumbled
His bumpy, wide body
Around the bend he grew
A giant boiling ball of molten lava
Up above the clouds he rumbles
Like an extremely fast washing machine that shakes.

### Finn Donnelly Smith (9)
St Peter's Catholic First School, Bromsgrove

# Mount Vesuvius

On the shore he guards
His beautiful, grateful town
Under the ground he shakes
His big, rocky body
In the distance he shakes
His huge, solid fireballs
Up in the sky he spits
His thin, long lava
Underground he shoots
His toxic eruption cloud.

## Zoe Pratt (9)
St Peter's Catholic First School, Bromsgrove

# Pompeii Discovery

Around the corner, the gigantic volcano was erupting fast
When the volcano erupted everyone was running quickly
In the house, everyone was scared because of the fierce shaky earthquake
In Pompeii, a city market was going on and something had been stolen!

### Billie-Rose Juggins (8)
St Peter's Catholic First School, Bromsgrove

# When I Grow Up

What do I want to do when I grow up?
Be an England footballer lifting the World Cup?
Perhaps I'll be a scientist working in a lab
Or I could learn to drive and get a taxicab?
I might want to be like Mum and Dad, do an office job
Nah, I'd rather be a rock star being adored by a mob.
Maybe an astronaut flying around the Earth
Or perhaps a midwife helping ladies to give birth?
I could be a dancer dancing around the stage
Or a tamer taming a lion in his circus cage?
I love animals, I could work in a zoo
Actually, I wouldn't like cleaning out the poo!
I'd like to drive a train or possibly a plane
Perhaps a doctor, helping people who are in pain?
I could be an explorer and travel over seas
Or be a police officer doing my duties
So many jobs to choose from, I wonder what I'll do
At least I don't have to decide yet, phew!

## Esme Stewart (8)
St Richard Reynolds Catholic College, Twickenham

# My Little Cat Archie

My little cat with golden fur
With a soft white belly and a soothing purr.
His little triangle ears,
From which he hears.
The tall, towering trees,
He digs his claws in and climbs with ease.
He's always up for a snuggle,
And he's the one you want to meet if you are looking for a cuddle.

My little cat so brave and loyal
Playfully bouncing around in the damp soil
In the garden, he chases the flyaway leaves
As he breathes in the fresh morning breeze
As the day draws to a close
He sprints across the grass
To meow at the glass
He gobbles down his food
And then trots upstairs in a lazy mood
At last, he'll slouch on a bed
To curl up in a little ball

And you won't hear another peep
For my little cat will be fast asleep.

## Elsie Kinch (9)
St Richard Reynolds Catholic College, Twickenham

# Panda Kisses

As I lie in bed there is something in my head
I don't know what it can be but it sure is bothering me.
Could it be a unicorn who wants to be my friend
Or a tiger who will eat me in the end?
Then I start to realise what it is
I think it is a panda who will give lots of kisses.
So I stay in bed and wait for it to come
But then I realise it's my sister being dumb.
Just then I finally see
A panda smiling at my sister and me.
I hope we will become best friends
With everlasting love that will not end.
I love you panda, yes I do
I will name you Little Blue
I will remember you wherever I go
Even if you don't so
You are special to me and I'm special to you
Oh my precious Little Blue.

## Lou Belloc (9)
St Richard Reynolds Catholic College, Twickenham

# The Solar System

**T** en million stars in the sky up high
**H** e stares at them every night
**E** very star so small to us

**S** o everyone makes a fuss
**O** h I just saw a shooting star
**L** et's sit back and look at these planets and stars so far apart
**A** star I think is cool
**R** epeat that and I will drool

**S** un is hot
**Y** et burns the planet's knot
**S** o that is what the sun is for
**T** o warm the planets to their core
**E** arth is my favourite planet
**M** y favourite star is a shooting star and it makes me want to speak Spanish.

## Amelia Nottage (8)
St Richard Reynolds Catholic College, Twickenham

# Goodbye Pepys

Pepys was the king of cats,
So say goodbye to your feather hats.

Pepys was a reading cat,
Named after a diarist so that is that.

Many a tale had he heard,
But never how to catch a bird.

Although he did kill lots of mice,
They came to our house more than twice.

The biggest cat you will ever see,
Took my bed, no room for me!

Unless out camping in his pot,
You could find him there more often than not!

Goodbye Pepys, I suppose he must have heard,
How to catch a bird.

He found it on a nearby street,
And there he lay fast asleep.

**Bosley Brown (10)**
St Richard Reynolds Catholic College, Twickenham

# A Moon Travel Lament

Once upon a time, the first man stood on the moon.
Then came more as the world was held spellbound.
Time moved on and the adventure finished too soon.
Will the children forever remain earthbound?

There it is, night after night.
Round, bright and glowing.
The place, a time before now, that started a race, no longer a fight.
Endeavour and curiosity for a generation, beyond our knowing.

In our lifetime, any more, no more, over too soon?
Our expedition completed to the silvery smiling man in the moon.

## Clemmie Needs (8)
St Richard Reynolds Catholic College, Twickenham

# My Star, Grandad

Good evening, Mr Moon
How are you this fine evening?
Thank you for lighting up the night sky
So we can see the stars!
Good evening, Grandad
Fourth star from the right of Mr Moon
Look, there you go shooting through the sky
Be careful, mind the other angels
Shine bright and keep a space next to you for me!
I miss you but I know when the sun sets
I will be able to see you shining bright
Your bright light reminds me of your smile
Shine bright, Grandad, love Alessandro.

## Alessandro Gasparini (8)
St Richard Reynolds Catholic College, Twickenham

# Miles Away Red Spot

My very embarrassed mother just sat upon nine pins
That rhyme I remember for the order the planets are in
If you sit upon this planet you will see the dazzling stars
The planet's not the colour but it's the name of a chocolate bar!
No oceans or mountains there but there's lots of wind and dust
If you really want to visit you'll need a rocket's thrust
It's a little ball of redness in the black of outer space
Like a burning ball of fire in a sooty fireplace.

## Lucy Enfys Enfys Birdseye (8)
St Richard Reynolds Catholic College, Twickenham

# Amazing Australia

**A** ustralia, a magical, mythical place for wildlife
**U** nbelievable places to discover and explore
**S** adly people had to evacuate because of bush fires
**T** o Reta, to Fremantle, to Sydney - everywhere's beautiful
**R** ush hour has barely any cars on the road
**A** ll the animals must love it there
**L** ovely weather makes it a pool day every day
**I** ncredible temperatures give you so much suntan
**A** nd I can't wait to go again.

## Finbar Harris (10)
St Richard Reynolds Catholic College, Twickenham

# Friendship

- **F** inding a good friend may not be east
- **R** espect and understanding will give it meaning
- **I** nspiring each other to be better
- **E** ncouraging your friends in times of need
- **N** ever giving up when doing a good dead
- **D** ependable friendship come rain or shine
- **S** upportive when times are bad
- **H** appy for them when they succeed
- **I** nstal confidence when they are nervous
- **P** artnership for today, tomorrow and forever.

## Sienna Minhas (9)
St Richard Reynolds Catholic College, Twickenham

# Book Lover

There once was a girl who couldn't stop reading
She read on her bed and she read on her ceiling
She read for days and weeks and months
She missed breakfast and supper and even brunch
She never blinked an eye when her mother called
She didn't move a muscle when her father pulled

One day as usual she sat reading in her bed
Her body as still as iron or lead
Suddenly she got a very funny feeling
But despite all this she carried on reading.

**Elisabeth Buxton (9)**
St Richard Reynolds Catholic College, Twickenham

# I Like Winter

**I** like to hurl snowballs
**L** ittle snowflakes fall and fill up the holes
**I** like to build snowmen
**K** ids like this game with old men
**E** veryone wants to go to Africa

**W** inter is as cold as Antarctica
**I** n winter you can go skiing
**N** othing is boring
**T** he ice skating is cool
**E** veryone wears wool
**R** ead, learn and love winter!

**Julia Szewczyk (9)**
St Richard Reynolds Catholic College, Twickenham

# Wildlife

W ildlife fills the skies and land
I n the rainforest, man turns tree to sand
L iving creatures big or small
D efying deforestation we should all stand tall
L ive for tomorrow and not for today
I n carbon reduction we should lead the way
F or our wildlife to survive we need a new beginning
E nsuring their survival gives the world its meaning.

## Liana Minhas (9)
St Richard Reynolds Catholic College, Twickenham

# Poor Penguins

- **P** enguins are adorable creatures
- **E** ach one has black and white features
- **N** ot every penguin gets food
- **G** laring at the seals who are very rude
- **U** ndermining the fact that they need to eat
- **I** t breaks my heart when they look down at their little feet
- **N** ow staying strong before they can be fed
- **S** o now they are lying in their little beds.

## Theo Corth (10)
St Richard Reynolds Catholic College, Twickenham

# The Wonderful Dream

As I close my eyes to sleep,
A wonderful dream is always there,
I see a hidden dimension full of wonder,
The beautiful sunlight shining down,
Wonderful creatures all around,
As birds soar through the sky like mystical phoenixes,
Here everyone is happy and free,
Certainly no plastic in the sea,
Incredible sights fill up my eyes with glee,
In this wonderful dream.

## Milo Ketteringham (9)
St Richard Reynolds Catholic College, Twickenham

# Go To The Park

**T** he park is a fun place to be
**H** appiness spreads to you and me
**E** lectronics shouldn't be allowed

**P** eople are around you, chatting face-to-face
**A** ny way people should have fun in the park
**R** iding on your scooter, bike or car
**K** indness is important like happiness so go the park!

## Annabelle Denizi (9)
St Richard Reynolds Catholic College, Twickenham

# The Night Journey

**R** oaring through the night skies
**A** ggressive flaming breath
**C** oughing hot smoke loudly
**I** nterrupting yellow eyes
**N** ow screeching through the black
**G** liding through the silence

**C** lawing through the air
**A** nd soon to vanish from this night
**R** acing its way home.

## Liam Pendleton (8)
St Richard Reynolds Catholic College, Twickenham

## Fabulous Fantastic Football

**F** ootball requires a special talent
**O** nly my dad knows all the skills
**O** bviously when I see him I am thrilled!
**T** ricks and skills help the team
**B** all control and scoring a goal
**A** s talented as Messi
**L** ove playing football with my dad
**L** eaves me happy, good and glad.

### Vic Mundow (9)
St Richard Reynolds Catholic College, Twickenham

# The Earth

The Earth is a little round ball
Where lots of children go to school
It is where you go to play
And where you laugh and sing all day
The gentle Earth that is blue and green
With danger everywhere that can't be seen
Our future is stolen and we are the thieves
Our little round ball, our children's dreams.

**Luke Doyle (9)**
St Richard Reynolds Catholic College, Twickenham

# Winter

**S** ave this crazy world from an icy-cold winter
**P** eople freezing in the chilly wind
**A** liens coming in all different colours like blue, green and red to help us
**C** hange our climate to live our amazing future in a happy way
**E** nvironment back to normal thanks to all the clever aliens from space.

## Euan John Fitzgerald-Monk (9)
St Richard Reynolds Catholic College, Twickenham

# Fears

**F** ears can come in all different ways like bullies and other stuff like that
**E** lectric buzzes shoot down your spine when you see your fear
**A** nxiousness can describe scared
**R** egaining strength to get over fears
**S** ome people have life-changing fears.

## James Hazerd (9)
St Richard Reynolds Catholic College, Twickenham

# Football

I get on the pitch
The sun's in my eyes
The whistle goes

Muddy, wet legs
The squelching grass
I get in place

The ball goes past
I feel more courage
Feel alive, proud, my team!

## Jemima Larmour (8)
St Richard Reynolds Catholic College, Twickenham

# Sports

Sports is really fun
I play it all day long in the summer sun
You can watch sports on the TV
But you can also watch it on CD
You see, sport is really fun
I would do it in the summer sun!

## Lily Rae Inch (9)
St Richard Reynolds Catholic College, Twickenham

# Space

The intergalactic space sloth
Wants to also be a moth
His mind is filled with intelligence
And he needs to find the word inheritance
My life is filled with wonder
While he gazes at the stars
When he tries he just goes to plunder
Although when he tries he can go to Mars
He likes to drink Irn-Bru
He gets nice and ready to watch some Doctor Who.

## Marcus Hall (10)
St Stephen's Catholic Primary School, Skipton

# Bullying

I don't know why they do it
The things they say hurt
They often pick on people
And they make you feel like dirt

They are often on the Internet
And pester people all day
Calling people names is their hobby
It's always got to be their way

If you are being bullied
Stay strong
Don't let them win
Their words and actions belong in the bin

Tell your parents
Or someone you trust
You don't have to put up with this
Talking about it is a must

For any bullies out there
What are you doing?

This is not okay
Yes you can make a change today

People are there to help
So take the opportunity
To improve yourself
And join a new community

We all need to work together
To make the world a better place
Let's make a change now
And forget all the rows.

**Oliver Butt (10)**
Stoke Park Primary School, Lockleaze

# Save The Earth

Dark days,
Come in many ways,
Nature can fill the sadness with happiness,
And we will all be happy again.

But,
If we have no nature,
We will all be in danger,
And we will all be dark forever.

Crumpled up leaves lie on the floor,
Chopped down trees and even more,
Save the Earth, save it now,
Then we will all be happy without a doubt.

Plastic in water,
Is pretty much torture
To the fish of wonder,
Who call it their home.

Saving the Earth,
Will give you heart,

So then the Earth,
Will not fall apart.

Trees wave their last goodbye,
And it makes you cry,
So sad you are,
You feel like an invisible ghost.

Burning down forests,
Wildfires,
Smoke rising,
From power plants and wires.

**Matilda Stringer (10)**
Stoke Park Primary School, Lockleaze

# Antonov An Mriya

Antonov, Antonov, you go in you go out
To airports and fly about
You see the sky and you see the clouds
You make people happy so go out.

Antonov, Antonov, you go out
You go into airports and fly about
I go in you
You take me and make me happy.

People take you because you are big and strong!
So Antonov, Antonov, you go out!

Antonov, Antonov, you are in Ukraine you are
So go out and fly to different countries.

Antonov, Antonov, people fly with you
So you're happy and the pilots support you.

Antonov An Mriya, I like you
So don't be afraid and go out with me!

**Teodor Mehedinti (10)**
Stoke Park Primary School, Lockleaze

# The Ruined Earth

We are killing the Earth
But people think it's fun
Nobody listens to us
Because we are young

Ask California
And see how they lost their homes
While world leaders
Just text on their phone

Floods covering the land
When will they take action?
Forests are burning down in a second
It ain't no attraction!

We all have a part to play
Speak up and join us to improve the world today.

### Alexis Hildich-Flay (10)
Stoke Park Primary School, Lockleaze

# Pets

Dogs are loving
They stop you from blubbing
They love to play
And they make your day.

Cats are precious
They follow you around
They become your shadow
And always turn a frown upside down.

Rabbits are friendly
They always want a cuddle
They become your best friend
And like to play in puddles.

Fish can be big
Fish can be small
They always swim around
And live in a glass bowl.

Pets are amazing
They teach you a lot of skills

They become part of your family
And give you a thrill.

## Georgia Lewis (9)
Stoke Park Primary School, Lockleaze

# Recycle The Rubbish

**R** espect the Earth in any way you can
**E** ven though it pulls you down
**C** all upon everyone you know, we all have a part to play
**Y** ou are responsible for helping the world
**C** ollecting bottles, recycling and picking up rubbish are just some of the things you can do
**L** isten to what's needed and lead the way
**E** veryone can start today and make the world a better place.

## Taylor Morris (10)
Stoke Park Primary School, Lockleaze

# Kindness

**K** eep a smile upon your face
**I** n every situation of the day
**N** ever leave your friends out of a game
**D** ecide to change someone's frown into a smile
**N** ever forget to care for the people around you
**E** veryone is a potential new friend
**S** o be kind to everyone you know
**S** uch a little smile can make everyone's day.

## Taja Thomas (10)
Stoke Park Primary School, Lockleaze

# The Two Sides

Sun, sun
Everyone loves sun
Come outside and have some fun
Everyone laughs and cheers
Come outside, the sun is here

Children climbing, children playing
They are having a great time here
But it starts to rain
So they go inside to play

Luckily the sun comes out again
But the children are addicted to video games!

## Leo Lloyd (9)
Stoke Park Primary School, Lockleaze

# Football

Football is a really good game
Many people play it for fame
Walford's club is on Park Street Lane
Man United's team fly on a plane

You could even play it in a hall
With a really, really flat ball
Sadio Mané's from Senegal
It is not dangerous at all.

**Ronnie Steele (10)**
Stoke Park Primary School, Lockleaze

# Bullying

**B** ullying is not cool
**U** psetting others hurts
**L** ook at their sad faces
**L** et's make a change!
**Y** ou have the power to stop!
**I** t's not good to be cruel
**N** o one wants to be mean to others
**G** o on, stop bullying.

**Courtney-Anne Slane (10)**
Stoke Park Primary School, Lockleaze

# Bullying

When you're mean how do you feel?
Why do you do this?
It makes me feel ill.

People ask you to stop
Yet you carry on
It brings me down
Yet I stay strong

Just no more bullying.

## William Butt (9)
Stoke Park Primary School, Lockleaze

# Spiders

**S** piders spin their silk
**P** roduce webs
**I** ntimidate people
**D** art around at night
**E** at flies
**R** ule over insects
**S** helter from the rain.

**Matt Hardy (9)**
Stoke Park Primary School, Lockleaze

# Solar System

I would like to see the solar system
I'm sure it would fill me with lots of wisdom
Mercury took the place of number one
The closest planet to the sun
Venus took place as number two
Shining bright like me and you
Earth is here at number three
This is where we live and breathe
Mars is our number four
I wouldn't want it at my door!
Jupiter's atmosphere you won't survive
But this gas giant's at number five
In at six is Saturn and her rings
Made of asteroids, ice and things
Uranus at seven and science agrees
If you were there you would freeze!
Neptune's eighth with fourteen moons
It reminds me of the harmony blues
The dwarf Pluto is last in line
And once was considered number nine!

## Dominic Norris (10)
Tany's Dell Primary School & Nursery, Harlow

# My Family

My family are the best
I do feel I am blessed
To have such a crazy bunch
They make my mind go crunch

Especially my little brother
Who makes my mind suffer
With all his silly pranks
I get left feeling a little blank

As for my little sister
She likes to dance like a hipster
She could go on the 'X Factor'
Because she is a really good actor

Now for mum and dad
We may make them go mad!
They are so trustworthy and kind
They are my sunshine

I do love my family
More than I can measure

They give me so many memories
That I will always treasure.

## Zoe Beck (9)
Tany's Dell Primary School & Nursery, Harlow

# The Small Mice

There are very small mice
And they are as small as a dice
The mice are as white as snow
And I had to tell them to go
When I got back
I said, "What is that?"
They told me that I was crazy
And then they went all lazy
They didn't know what to do
But after that, they got the flu
I said, "There's nothing I can do!"
Just then I saw them as they flew
They flew away to explore, what I cannot say
After they had flown away
They came back to say
"When you feel fine
Never eat a lime!"

## Amber Mitchell (10)
Tany's Dell Primary School & Nursery, Harlow

# My Friend

Before I met you I was so lonely
But knowing you Leon makes me so lucky
Friendship is like magic, it makes you happy
It wipes tears and brings smiles
Being side by side and holding hands
No more sorrowful days and hello joyful days

Our memories are like bright stars in the night sky
Our adventures are like exciting events in a fairy-tale story
Our dreams fly so high like birds in the wide sky
I can't wait for more cosy memories
I am looking for more crazy adventures
So stay by my side and tightly hold my hand.

**Homam Eizeddin (9)**
Tany's Dell Primary School & Nursery, Harlow

# Harry Potter's Journey

Harry Potter's uncle was very mean
But Hagrid was so keen
To get Harry into the magical world
The shops of wands and brooms blew him away
But Malfoy came and ruined his day
He made lots of amazing friends
Learnt potions and spells that would never end
Then Harry met his worst nightmare
His name was Voldemort, he had no hair
He made them think he was going to die
But then he opened one eye
Everyone was astonished by his bravery
Harry defeated Voldemort finally.

## Summer Parkin (9)
Tany's Dell Primary School & Nursery, Harlow

# Best Friends Till The End

I've got your back, you have got mine,
I'll help you out. Any time!
To see you hurt, to see you cry,
Makes me weep and wanna die.
And if you agree to never fight,
It wouldn't matter who's wrong or right.
If a broken heart needs a mend,
I'll be right there until the end.
If your cheeks are wet from drops of tears,
Don't worry, let go of your fears.
Hand in hand,
Love is sent.
We'll be best friends...
Till the end!

## Lili Mai Turner (10)
Tany's Dell Primary School & Nursery, Harlow

# Football Day

One Sunday morning when the football starts
When the whistle blows like a girl screaming they begin
Clandon vs Chesant
Mark had the ball
It was the rule
Because no other went for it
Freddie said, "Wow!" at Mark's football skills
*Boom!*
One-nil to Clandon
Ollie had the ball
Not for long
Ollie said, "Nooo!"
Near to the end, Freddie shot
Full-time whistle
All shaking hands
Final score one-nil.

## Mark White (10)
Tany's Dell Primary School & Nursery, Harlow

# The Python

I'm a little python small and fat
People who know me like to call me Pat

I sleep in the day and stay awake all night
Be careful where you walk or I will give you a fright!

My mum is long and thin
This is because she chases around the bin

My dad is big and brave
Because his mum left him in a cave

Please don't touch me as I may bite
So just sit back and watch me as I sit there with all my might.

### Nathan Madge (9)
Tany's Dell Primary School & Nursery, Harlow

# Stages Of My Life

I am a girl
I really like pearls
If I were a boy
I would probably like toys
When I am a little bit older
I'll be even braver and bolder
When I'm a lady
I probably still won't like gravy
If I were a man
I would like to drive a van
When I am a grandma
I would like a pamper
If I was a grandad
I would probably drive myself mad
Until then I will just be me
Fun-loving, kind and free.

**Lottie Waites (9)**
Tany's Dell Primary School & Nursery, Harlow

# Skittles' Adventures

Once there was a pig named Skittles
Who loved to eat pickles
But one day he could not find pickles for teddy
Who was named Wickles
She went to go look in Forest Sprinkles
She went to go look behind for Twinkle
But he wasn't there
So she went to go look in Castle Air
And there he was, sitting on a chair
She went back to sit in her zone
She fell asleep happy
Then the rest of the day she felt wacky.

**Darcy Rowlandson (10)**
Tany's Dell Primary School & Nursery, Harlow

# Hogwart's Poem

Hogwarts is a mystical place,
Harry Potter fits in with the scar upon his face.
The Chamber of Secrets has many warnings,
To Harry who has visions until the morning.
Hogwarts has a lot of spells like 'expecto patronum',
But a lot of spells means, well... a lot of plot twists that are parallel!
And Harry was told by Hagrid that he was a wizard
Who's told by Voldemort that he is just a kid.

## Ruby Kings (10)
Tany's Dell Primary School & Nursery, Harlow

# Cheeky Little Arthur

My cheeky little Arthur,
As silly as can be,
He really loves me,
From what I see,
He is very sneaky,
With a bark that is squeaky,
Arthur is as cheeky as a monkey,
But is really funky,
He's a bit chunky,
He is as cute as a model,
He should be in a novel,
His fur is brown,
And he never has a frown,
I love Arthur the way he is,
And I am grateful for this.

## Beau Cruickshank (9)
Tany's Dell Primary School & Nursery, Harlow

# The Girl That Played Football

The girl that played football
Her dream to be had
The girl that played football
Played football with her dad
The girl that played football
Oh how the boys all laughed
The girl that played football
Had the last laugh
Wembley, Wembley, here she comes
England's number one
One goal, two goals, three goals, four
This superstar will always score!

**Chloe Nash (9)**
Tany's Dell Primary School & Nursery, Harlow

# Tech Me Back

My mum used to play outside with a ball
Now everyone sits inside the same four walls

My dad used to ride around on his bike
Now all anyone wants is Facebook likes

My grandad used to play in the woods with his pals
Now everybody stays indoors in their house

Technology has changed us, that's for sure
Let's all communicate a little more!

**Jack Wiggins (9)**
Tany's Dell Primary School & Nursery, Harlow

# Loki

My dog is so lazy and sleeps most of the day
He curls up on my lap and gets his own way
He's happy to see me when I come down the stairs
His fur is soft and silky but he drops a lot of hairs
He likes long walks and tires me out
And sometimes he's mighty and makes me shout
But he's my best friend and I love him so
I never ever ever want Loki to go.

**Alex Theodorou (9)**
Tany's Dell Primary School & Nursery, Harlow

# Blobby's Dreams From Mars

He's green and hairy bouncing all around
Swinging on the swing at the Mars' playground
Dreaming, wishing he could just take flight
Just like those astronauts flying through the night
One day maybe he will get to go
To the blue and green planet and travel around the globe
Keep dreaming until the very end
One day maybe will you be Blobby's friend?

**Abigail Jones (9)**
Tany's Dell Primary School & Nursery, Harlow

# The Colours Of Nature

Red is my cheeks on a cold winter's day
Orange is autumn leaves crunching under my boots
Yellow is the sun beating down on the beach
Green is the leaves sparkling in the morning sunlight
Blue is the sky above my head
Indigo is the sun fading in the evening sky
Violet is the flowers blooming in spring
I love all the rainbow colours.

## Sophia Mckenzie (10)
Tany's Dell Primary School & Nursery, Harlow

# Save The Turtles

There once was a turtle called Murtle
Who lived in the deep blue sea
When one day Murtle
Could not see!
As her head was stuck in a can
Murtle was one of the lucky
Ones who were set free
By a kind man

That's how turtles
Get hurt
When you don't clean up the sea

Save the turtles!

## Daisy Smiins (10)
Tany's Dell Primary School & Nursery, Harlow

# Mother Nature!

The day was bright,
The winds were light,
All of the leaves were swirling in flight,
The sky was as hazy as a summer night,
You could feel the soft breeze as it came into night,
As the day ended the brightness did fade,
All over the sky,
You could see the beautiful stars in the moonlight sky.

**Teegan Ayers (9)**
Tany's Dell Primary School & Nursery, Harlow

# My Family

We mostly live together,
We care for each other,
Even if naughtier,
Like friends forever.

Punishment boring,
Education strong,
Learning is fun,
One by one.

We're all one big family,
With ups and downs every day,
That is our family
Ready to stay.

### Oliver Telfer-Maleary (10)
Tany's Dell Primary School & Nursery, Harlow

# Friendship

Oh what a joy it is to have a friend like you
For giving me strength the way you do
For lifting me up when I am feeling down
For putting a smile on my face when I'm wearing a frown
Thanks for being there and helping me grow
Your friendship means a lot, this I would like you to know.

## Logan Hodgson (9)
Tany's Dell Primary School & Nursery, Harlow

# Crazy Stuff In Ballet

Once there was a girl named Mae
Then she went to ballet
After that she went to play
Then saw Santa in his sleigh
After that she screamed, "Yay!"
But she felt really grey
Then she was told to stay
But she smelt so she had a spray
Then went home and had some hay.

**Lacie Arrowsmith**
Tany's Dell Primary School & Nursery, Harlow

# Football

This game will give you a thrill
In summer or autumn's chill
Popping pads and pounding feet
Will lead us to an opponent's defeat
A taste of sweat hit after hit
The defence never quit
Move that ball and always run
Let's show our supporters who is number one.

**Ronnie Fry (9)**
Tany's Dell Primary School & Nursery, Harlow

# The Night Sky

The stars at night start from light
Travelling along they light the night sky
Sometimes the night clouds block your view
On a clear night we see a twinkle from you

When the sun comes your light fades away
But I know you will be back at the end of the day.

**Keira Rooney (9)**
Tany's Dell Primary School & Nursery, Harlow

# A Snowy Day

I was making cookie dough
It was really small though
I saw a snowball on its way
And thought, q*uick get on your sleigh!*
I was skating down the hill with my friend
But we hit a bump
It made us jump
And then we shouted, "Weeeeee!"

## Ruby Richardson (9)
Tany's Dell Primary School & Nursery, Harlow

# The Magic Of Friendship

Friendship is magical and extraordinary
Friendship is priceless
Best friends are rare
Good friends always care
Best friends are always filled with wonderful and helpful advice
Best friends are the best at encouraging you into things.

## Renée Smith (10)
Tany's Dell Primary School & Nursery, Harlow

# The Old Nun

I once turned into a crippled old nun
I killed just for fun
I discovered a man and used a cunning plan
I used my bait and took him on a date
Made him scream and run
That was the story of the dumb old nun!

## Marcus Myers Evans (10)
Tany's Dell Primary School & Nursery, Harlow

# Splat Goes The Pizza Dough

Once I made some pizza dough
Then I threw it up and said, "Oh no!
Watch out below!"
Then it landed on my toe
So I had to go get some more pizza dough!

**Charlie Collier (9)**
Tany's Dell Primary School & Nursery, Harlow

# Nature

I see the clouds, I watch them go
The river drifts, I watch it flow
Flowers bloom, I watch them grow
Nature's beautiful, but does it know?

I see the sun, I watch it glow
Birds tweet, they say hello
Leaves fall, I watch them blow
Nature's beautiful, but does it know?

**Ava Lane (8)**
Temple Mill Primary School, Strood

# Rain Go Away

The sun goes away
As the rain comes to play
The rain is angry today
As the animals explore
They open their jaws
*Pitter-patter, pitter-patter*
*Tat, tat, tat, tat*
In their mouth
Whilst they travel south
The boys and girls
Do some twirls
It helps them forget
About the rain
It pours hard
Like a bucket of water
Tipped on your hand.

## Watkins (9)
Turners Hill CE Primary School, Turners Hill

# Galaxy

Black is dead but space is wild,
A thousand planets flying by.
On this speck of one, a child,
Staring wide-eyed at the sky.

Stars dancing to the tune of God,
Swirling in their gowns of fire.
With the wings of an angel,
Dance they do to Heaven's choir.

Planets passing one by one,
Made of rings and ice and snow.
Nine of them around the sun,
With mysteries we've never known.

**Jessica Meadows (9)**
Wivelsfield Primary School, Wivelsfield

# Crisps, Crisps, Crisps!

Tasty crisps, salty crisps,
Crunchy, curvy crispy crisps
Don't stop until finished crisps
Those are the ones I like
Delicious crisps, delightful crisps
Little brittle crumbly crisps
Have a treat on Friday crisps
Those are the ones I like

Snapping crisps, cracking crisps,
Cheesy, chilli onion crisps
Have some in your lunch box crisps
Those are the ones I like
Munching crisps, crunching crisps
Pretty popping party crisps
Buy some for a bargain crisps
Those are the ones I like.

**Ilyas Widrig (8)**
Yorkmead Primary School, Hall Green

# Believe In Yourself

Life may be tough
Things will get rough
There will be bad days
It may seem like a haze

Believe in yourself and in your dream
Though impossible things may seem
Someday, somehow, you will get through
The good you have in view

Paint your mind
And guide your thoughts
Share the amazing achievements
And think about your faults

Try your best
And you won't wonder
What you have done
You past the level of thunder.

**Krishna Tank (9)**
Yorkmead Primary School, Hall Green

# Imagine, Imagine

Imagine, imagine
Standing at the tip of Mount Everest

Imagine, imagine
You change something by a bit
But that bit
Had a colossal meaning

Imagine, imagine
Everybody follows you till
Their very last breath

Imagine, imagine
You won the Nobel prize!

Imagine, imagine.

**Kritika Tank (9)**
Yorkmead Primary School, Hall Green

# YOUNG WRITERS INFORMATION

We hope you have enjoyed reading this book – and that you will continue to in the coming years.

If you're a young writer who enjoys reading and creative writing, or the parent of an enthusiastic poet or story writer, do visit our website **www.youngwriters.co.uk**. Here you will find free competitions, workshops and games, as well as recommended reads, a poetry glossary and our blog. There's lots to keep budding writers motivated to write!

If you would like to order further copies of this book, or any of our other titles, then please give us a call or order via your online account.

Young Writers
Remus House
Coltsfoot Drive
Peterborough
PE2 9BF
(01733) 890066
**info@youngwriters.co.uk**

Join in the conversation!
Tips, news, giveaways and much more!

**YoungWritersUK**   **@YoungWritersCW**